Scars

Pitt Poetry Series

Also by Peter Meinke

FICTION
The Piano Tuner, 1986

POETRY
The Night Train and the Golden Bird, 1977
Trying to Surprise God, 1981
Night Watch on the Chesapeake, 1987
Liquid Paper: New and Selected Poems, 1991

POETRY CHAPBOOKS
Lines from Neuchâtel, 1974
The Rat Poems, 1978
Underneath the Lantern, 1986
Far from Home, 1989
Campocorto, 1996

CHILDREN'S VERSE
The Legend of Larry the Lizard, 1969
Very Seldom Animals, 1970

CRITICISM
Howard Nemerov, 1968

Scars

Peter Meinke

University of Pittsburgh Press

Published by the University of Pittsburgh Press, Pittsburgh, Pa. 15260
Copyright © 1996, Peter Meinke   5/3/97.
All rights reserved
Manufactured in the United States of America
Printed on acid-free paper
10   9   8   7   6   5   4   3   2   1

Library of Congress Cataloging-in-Publication data and acknowledgments
will be found at the end of this book.

A CIP catalog record for this book is available from the British Library.
Eurospan, London

The publication of this book is supported by grants from the National Endowment for the Arts in Washington, D.C., a Federal agency, and the Pennsylvania Council on the Arts

For our parents:
Kathleen McDonald Lewis, Harry Frederick Meinke,
Ruth Havens Clark, Roger Philips Clark

Contents

III. The Square Root of Love

E-Mail from Tokyo

> They fuck you up, your mum and dad
> They may not mean to, but they do.

Today we received Tim's letter dated tomorrow
so in a sense we can reply before it's written
which is how we'd always like to deal with our children:
Look inside your lovely heads and get there before you

Dear children by now we have all devoured Larkin
and so are terrified at the half-truth imbedded
in his lines: the passing on of damage like coded
messages we can't decipher till the battle's done

and we've all lost   It's true that tendencies to panic
or weep or show off seem to run in the family
and I apologize for this   Weakness for whisky
is in there as well bad eyes and hypochondriac

twitches (my shoulder throbs as I write this)   We know friends
who won't have kids at all because the world's meaner and
more complex   Just look around   they tell us   Who can stand
it?   *We can*   I answer *and we'd do it all again*

because our memories wrap around the four of you
like the thick Amish quilts we brought home from Ohio
one for each of you   spreading them in a royal row
and guessing correctly in advance which ones you'd choose

Philosophical despair 'ain't worth a row of pins'
your Grandma would have told you   *Have children of your own*
is our advice   So you throw yourself to the unknown
gambling with your life and theirs: *Well that's what living means*

I know what memory and poetry need: storm   moon
dolphin   eye   strings of images strung like those four kites
across a summer sky years ago the wind snapping
letters toward the sun   *Kiss me*   *Dear one*   *Stay safe*   *Write soon*

but in the end we can only cry your names sending
them skyward fragile and flammable affirming that
you're ours (poor babies):   Perrie   Peter   Gretchen and at
last thanking you for tomorrow's letter   Timothy

I   Scars

A Debate on Determinism

She was chosen because
she was beautiful
physiognomy is all
so she stole the ball

He barely knew how to dance
which had no consequence since
family is everything
and he was a prince

She dressed in tatters till
her fairy godmother showed
it's who you know
that matters

At midnight the coach
turned pumpkin at her approach
this was hard but *ripeness is all*
proclaimeth the bard

Puzzling: it seems
for the purpose of predicting
from lackey to king
everything is everything

Well the prince found her finally
at the end of the block
what luck!
at last they could fuck

learning too late
he hated small feet
but such is our lot:
you can't escape fate

Emily Dickinson in Hell

How flat — as a Democracy —
I wondered   entering
and seeing row on ragged row
unrav'ling like a sleeve

with no distinctions or — demands
to pry the fearful eye
and none but Weather hanging there
across an absent sky

I looked for instruments and coal
machines whose teeth reflect
a terrifying gleam — to those
who suffer from Defect

I looked for friends or enemies
but only sapless trees
breathed meagerly in Emptiness
between the heated seas

until I shrieked in Agony
beneath a sycamore —
and peered deep in its branches
to find my Father — there

Scars

When I was young I longed for scars
like my father's   They were the best
scars on the block startling varied
pink as a tongue against his whiskey skin

The longest bolted from his elbow
finger-thick where the barbed wire plunged in
a satin rip thinning toward the wrist
I read the riddle of my father's body

like a legend punctuated by pale hyphens
neat commas surgical asterisks and exclamation
points from scalp to ankle   His tragic knuckles
spoke violence in demotic Greek

My silent father said little too little it seems
but after the divorce he told me tracing
the curved path on his skull where hair never grew
'It's the ones you can't see that kill you'

and it's true our doctor said his liver
which did him in was scarred like an old war-horse
Still the mark I knew best I gave him myself   hitting
a pop fly straight up and swinging the child's bat again

with all my might as the ball descended
over the plate   He had run in to catch it
and the bat cracked him under his chin dropping
my father like a murdered king peeling a wound

no butterfly bandage could cover   I was too stunned
to move but the look my mother gave me proved
no matter what happened later this man bleeding
like Laius on the ground was the one she loved

Ice

The only thing I can remember my father teaching me
is how to carry an ice tray without spilling:
Keep your eye on the front compartment he'd say *you'll see*

it works: not a blessèd drop lost Fortunately
that's a practical lesson I've been more than willing
to follow every day of my life so I think of him fondly

as I pad back&forth making ice for our martini
ritual Mom shrilled from her pulpit *Those are killing*
you you know and she was dead-on right but he

didn't care nor do we an inherited suicidal tendency
like a toothpick in the blood his stoic shrug drilling
into us the appeal of containing your own catastrophe

Peter he'd smile holding out his glass remember Gethsemane
was an olive grove and I'd think of the disciples milling
about and Jesus waiting for Judas beside an olive tree

and despite my name as I fixed him his drink with its three
olives I wondered which one was me in the kitchen swilling
gin with my sick old man waiting for him to say as I picked up the tray
Keep your eye on the front compartment: You'll see

Reading at Night

Unable to sleep I read
in the old wingback chair
in our living room
lone lamp burning

Peering above my book I find
framed in the tall window
a portrait by Vermeer
all blue and gold

the ornate lampshade's glow
the indigo base
and half-illuminated
like a mask an old man's face:

it is my uncle's face
my mother's brother
with its high puzzled
forehead pointed chin

and ragged moustache
struggling to be bold
When had he slipped in
to take my place?

I saw him only twice
after our parents' harrowing
divorce   I don't know
if he was strong or kind

or wise yet here he is
inside me or outside although
looking closer I can see
my father's sad accusing eyes

The Vietnamese Fisherman on Tampa Bay

Two hundred yards from the Navy ship
a school of whiting zigzags through the bay
baby torpedoes on the prowl for prey
until near the shore where businessmen sip
their drinks they snap at a rubber shrimp run
by their eyes and feel their world go blind
and dry flipping and gasping on the ground
beside the Vietnamese fisherman

He stands feet spread apart without a pole
only a line with hook and shrimp he flicks
with an awkward throw like an old slow-pitch
pitcher at a picnic   It goes
maybe twenty thirty feet: then hand
over hand he guides the line toward shore until
with a quick snap of his thin brown wrists
he hooks another whiting pulls and lands

it near the sign: Keep Off the Grass we think
he can't read English   But he's one hell
of a fisherman: no one else
catches anything worth keeping while sleek
whiting quiver in his pail   He can feed
an extended family tonight . . .   Last month
we all remember four Asian boys in fun
trespassed above the Navy station (No Swimming!

the sign shouts) and one by one marched out
sinking like toy soldiers seen by a neighbor
from a house across the street racing over
he saved the last while the mother howled . . .
Here at lunch no one says *gook* We speculate
on war and peace: Do all our Vietnamese
know each other?   Are they all lost cousins
in this bleached city far from Tonkin Bay?

Near the fisherman a boy we guess his child
digs with a stick steady as a mole
burrowing to China   Beside the hole
a fish snaps like a patient gone wild
in electric shock   Compared to microphones
and disks our world of stocks and portable
computers the scene looks elemental
solid the tattered players more composed

than we natty in blazers suits and ties
Our work seems artificial chintzy
as plastic pink flamingos   Fishing
and digging Bill says at least are real   I try
to imagine coming home at end of day
with a bucket of fish   *Fishing is real*
I'll tell them *Whiting sea trout mackerel* . . .
No shit Ho Chi Minh our kids will say

. . . Back in the building from its vestibule
we can still see the pair of them father
and son only their arms moving the flare
of light from the fish popping like flashbulbs
There's little we can do or have undone
experience is one and one and one
The coast is crowded now sweet grassland tarred
the soothing languor of habit rocks our home
a pelican by the seawall drops down low
an anhinga spreads his wings out like a god . . .

Anthills

It's true that my soul mea culpa is empty
but maybe it's supposed to be empty   Maybe
it's more like a monk's cell than a Victorian
living room   In the darkness I scratch a line on
my soul's bare wall meaning One more day scratch the son
of a bitch *off* So that's what life means: *One more day*
Not very enlightening but what am I a

Roman candle like Virgil singing 'Arms and the
Man'?   My grandma crocheted doilies that were always
floating off the arms of our overstuffed chairs and
sofas like huge soiled snowflakes   *To pass the day* she
said I'm more like Grandma than Virgil praise the saints
(she'd say) though I hope I don't get cancer   The pills
erased her mind like a tape: children grandchildren
all those doilies vanished as if she had never

pressed them to her breast   Nothing left but pills and tubes

We all need a gardener named Guido to shoot us
before it's too late   When I scratch my wall I try
to scratch it deep little heaps of powdered cement
along the wall like so many anthills or mole-
hills or mountains it doesn't much matter does it:
we're talking about meaning here   Outside my cell
the hand is on the throat the bullet squints in its
chamber the victory song screeches like a hawk

Roll off the names: Rwanda Bosnia Yemen
Waco Haiti Cambodia Los Angeles
No one knows anything bodies piling up like
anthills molehills . . . We may not be able to save
or predict or teach or even please anymore
but at least each line should testify under oath
under God (undercut underground):   *we can count*

The Parade

Honolulu 1993

. . . feeling it in our feet before we saw it
or even heard it: the big bass drum
of the Fourteenth Army Battalion thumping
after the Manoa High School float
In Praise of Lasting Peace those irresistible
children waving Aloha to all of us
at curbside the drum corps busting
down the boulevard behind them *its* call

also irresistible as if to say
body and mind are neatly split
the need to embrace the instinct to hit
like incompatible couples who stay
together for the sake of the child
The soldiers' boots glittered eyes
and faces blackened to disguise
their sweet youthfulness & the wild

drums picked up their step and coarsened
their voices while they cried:
We're the boys of Company B your right
your left the crowd roaring
when they surged past under the snapping flag
until the next float rolled by with a pretty girl
singing 'Sweet Leilani' as if the world
whirled only for love   Trade winds dragged

soft clouds above us holding the dark clouds
in the distance and I thought of how drums
were made of skin stretched tight over some
sort of emptiness   and how
they affected me who want in my heart
nothing but peace: but when the drums beat
my hair comes to attention and my bones bark at me
to stand up like a man & march . . .

13

The Triumph of Desert Storm

. . . out of the blue horses'
steam rose like strings
as if they had been lowered into morning
by a great puppeteer leaning
above scrub pine and cedar
on my uncle's farm near Ocala

O and those horses towered
above me like skyscrapers even at a distance
and my young eyes bore me bareback
soaring over Florida sand
below the white sun breasting
toward us through moss and mist

And below me the country
unrolled in a sweet pure
patchwork of abstract art
green and brown and yellow around
the still sparkling stars
of my father's cities . . .

Well this is a way to begin a poem
fairly easily tapping in
to the unconscious and leaping toward some
unrhymed memory or random invention
while even as we dream the homeless stir
beneath the *Times* on Central Avenue
morning kicking toward them like an officer
with notched nightstick and thick boots

The papers already brittle torn spotted
crackle and crow: *100,000 Iraqis*
slaughtered!   spitting on proportion truth
a generation ruined and rotting
in the Gaza of our inner cities
and the tall blue horses of our youth

14

Organ Recital, April 19, 1995

for R.V.S.

CHARITY spread its letters above the herringbone
brickwork of St. Paul's Chapel light flaking off trumpet
and the tall torpedoes of the organ pointing down

while the schoolgirls bent with glowing eyes to their duet
in C Minor inspired by youth and Mendelssohn
to bring us midday amnesty at 116th Street

in Manhattan spring exactly at the moment when

Oklahoma City changed forever and I thought
not knowing things were different now of men and women
I went to school with who are gone: *Bob Stone Gordie Raitt*

Priscilla Willard the list swelling like an ocean
in a storm   It stabs the heart the damage is so great
as we sink with music's arms around us till we drown

Chinese Wish Poem

for James Nolan

Brinda said Jimmy said
Write your true wish on this paper
burn it and sure as smoke winds
like a monkey up a tree this wish
comes true

Well why not?   All my life I've
ducked making wishes each year blew
out candles squeezing my eyes
blue & unbelieving pretending
to wish

but this is the Year of Good
Fortune a chance to renew
the old dance when nothing's new
or bright even the nearby bay
gone stale

fish turning up in the tide like
bad cards   So I'll make that wish
Not for happiness though: who
cares who needs it who sniffs it
like glue?

World peace?   But we have some fine
revolutions still to go   Long life?
Old age looms stupid as an ox   Health
and sex the physical things?   I'd have
a *few*

good wishes there: *some* things I'd like
to do and haven't tried as yet   Still
they seem trivial somehow and then
I thought of art one consolation we
can do

16

in a diminished time: to write a beau-
tiful song   But even as I brought my pen
to page the worm inside my head turned yet again
hissing *Everything's selfish especially*
Beauty . . .

so I think and think and finally write
my wish light it the flames chewing
through rice paper toward the red
and gold figures and my heart's ink:
I ask to die before our children die

17

Noreen

In any group there are the beautiful and
the plain the strong & weak smart as a trinket
& dumb as a clam   Agreed   But there's little
agreement who they are or correlation
with how they all turn out   Noreen here lying

on the storeroom floor with her head on a sack
of potatoes phone dangling from the wall and
a plastic cup of vodka on the shelf was
voted Wittiest in the Class and the Girl
with the Nicest Eyes   *Where be your gibes now?* asked

Hamlet as indeed did Noreen when playing
Hamlet in ninth grade pronouncing it *guybs* while
Miss Endicott rolled her eyes which weren't half
as nice as Noreen's   Outside it's been dead cold
and rainy for a month and polluted air

gums your glasses like snails the ink smears on her
lover's letter   *Dear Noreen*   For years she has
held the wrong job the wrong man   She even had
the wrong child   Those are the reasons   How much we
need reasons!   How reasons make us feel better!

Still Life, 1988

Three objects say an apple pear and vase
can pose perfection in a work of art
but any three people in any one place

frame the wrong tension lines start
breaking up: this the difference between
likeness and life   Ripe apple-shape apart

is boring the added pear makes it seem
balanced but static: so the vase completes
the circuit each one's energy streaming

toward the other: the artist in his or her sweet
ecstasy leans back and thinks Done!
and calls it . . . *Still Life, 1988* . . .

but that same artist be it Joan or John
has two good friends and if they were
as they're bound to be arranged in one

room long enough something will start to stir
in John or Joan and split his pear-shaped heart or hers

Goalfish

are nomadic slipping
sideways through shallows in tight
schools along shoreline breaks
to some warm shady weedbed
of our lake

They're serious these goal-
fish mouths frowning like bankers
heads shaking eyes round as
nickels   *This is serious*
serious

When young the sweet darters
make easy prey greengold scales
glinting like Spanish coins
translucent tails signaling
Swallow me

to the big fish cruising
and cashing in near deep holes
In winter even their
parents eat them as they flick
back and forth

under rock and dock   If
they survive growing bars from
belly to fin they'll do
the same to their own fry sons
and daughters

until time to move on
and they weave across borders
among hooks angling like
untranslated questions to
the slack at the end of the line . . .

Spanish Moss

for Tim

Storm-shaken your plane circles on hold over
Tampa Bay   We know but don't say 'the lightning
center of America'   Bolts whack the runway
like a judge's gavel drinks rock on the table
Modern we're too shy to pray so we talk about . . .
Spanish moss how it gets wet and heavy
in the rain pruning our oak trees   When
we get home holding you safe between us branches
will twist knee-deep around the house the moss
clumped like seaweed on our *have you changed*

have you grown are you frightened do you love us
When you were young you liked to be scared
by the moss coiling under the moon along
the snaky live oak limbs how your eyes widened
when the wind roiled the Bay by our house
and we would explain lightning the negative charge
from a cloud leaping to the positive charge
of its shadow at how many million feet per second
the flash beating the rumble because light races
faster than *are you happy is she with you are*

you healthy did you miss we are six years
older practicing for death the ultimate diet
no more cheesecake no more chocolate no more fat
alcohol reserved for stress and celebration
and since this is both I believe I'll have another
Spanish moss doesn't really kill trees the balled
moss is worse the hanging kind just blocks the sun
youcansprayitwithliquidcopperbut
that stuff can *where is that plane is the pilot*
sober when we outgrow this trembling will you remember?

Quick Off the Mark

I know a man who never did much
but keeps the clippings of his small victories
folded in plastic in his pocket
Buy him a drink or meet him for lunch
and you'll hear his stories:
class president winning basket
medals for Spanish and French

It's a question of growing up:
We all yearn to be quick off the mark
sleek and desirable
from sixth grade on each group
a test each neighborhood each block
eachpartyeachteameachdate all
measuring pressuring saying: *Shape up*

But we never can: never enough!
Deaf and battered as baby seals
we don't learn how to lose or even try
second place with its bric-a-brac of
inadequacy   Wrapped in unreal
fur we slither and writhe
in polar circles trying to slip it off

because if we don't it's the loony bin
the bullet in the head
or the megalomaniac hip-hipping
in triumph over everyone
over people like my friend
unfolding his creased clippings
with a grin and a gin

How our souped-up gung-ho America
needs to rearrange its ideas
of victory and defeat to ponder
imperfection
whose complex beauty flowers
like the silversword from cinder
and rock on Mount Haleakala:

we simply must grow up   . . . But still
unbidden I see myself at fifteen on first
base   They try and miss picking me off
and the silver voice of Priscilla Willard
cries *You'll never get him!*   On the very next
pitch they pick me off:
an early sign that all will not go well . . .

Blow, Blow, Thou Winter Wind

Then heigh-ho the holly, this life is so jolly!

In my criminal stage I fell in love with Bert
who did an awkward handstand in her skirt
that sent the Sage girls gasping from the room
This was the fifties life could be shocking then
and I lived like a pig in the college dorm
reserved for Jews and other exiles   Bert moved in

on weekends   A Polish boozer in
love and hate with God she'd mime His voice: *Bert
hast thou dropped thine pants again?   Thou die!*   The dorm
hall echoed as she trilled slipping her skirt
and shoes and jumping on the bed then
calling for wine or vodka as if my room

were some East Village den   In truth the room
was smoky sticky vile sweatshirts festered in
dank mounds ashtrays stank   She'd flip the stolen thin-
stemmed glass over her thin shoulder   Bert
liked to think we had a fireplace   Later we'd skirt
the shards of glass in our bare feet blow the dorm

and saunter through the snow while half the dorm
hung out their windows cheering   There wasn't room
for coyness in our act: she'd flap her wet skirt
back at them take my arm and heads high in
we'd go crashing some Christmas party where Bert
would lean on the piano while I cadged drinks   Then

pure as any Shakespeherian maid sing *Then
heigh-ho, the holly!*   under a lion dorm-
ant on a shield: *Semper liber*   Ah Bert
you were beautiful in those heraldic rooms
your long-lashed umber eyes drowning in
music   And I would clown sprawled before your skirt

24

your bare toes tapping out beneath that skirt
their fragile SOS a neurasthen-
ic code I hopelessly misread seeing in-
stead only your fine frenzy   If later in the dorm
you curled weeping in my arms the room
tight with shadows I should have whispered *Bert*

although this squalid dormitory room
squats in the skirts of hell your presence here
is holy   Bert God loves us now and then

Labels, 1972

That year we collected wine labels
because they were pretty and wine
was new for us sophisticated
a step up from a can of Bud
or a shot of whatever whiskey
we found on sale   Our favorite
was *Oeuil de Perdrix* a rosé

whose label sported a chestnut-
colored bird with a red tail
We steamed it off and glued it
on a lampshade and still today
when Neuchâtel seems farther
than Tibet that bird glows
in the night above my desk

even while I sleep especially
while I sleep calling
in partridge *Fly fly*
with me to the steep slope
of the Jura the wide lake
the clustered vine laden
with such promise the sweet grapes!

Unnatural Light

After the break-in
we hung spotlights on the garage outside
Light-sensitive they flare on at dusk
fade out at dawn night-blooming suns
on crime watch

Through the dense dark
light pulses under oak and laurel
pulling the stems of periwinkle and begonia
the crimson bougainvillea on the trellis
the calamondin with its bitter fruit
When the wind blows in their shadows
slide like burglars along the wall
beyond our barred windows
around the shaky birdhouse
spilling crumbs

And the white azaleas confused
by so much light confess their startling secrets
three months early   The others farther out
huddle in natural darkness playing it safe
keeping mum

Steroids

for Frank Dreisbach

Nature wants to make a race of it
on her own: the fibers of our skin

reknit and bloom blood clears film
on the eye scatters like torn tickets

at Belmont   But when the forced food hits
and your muscles swell thighs slick

as thoroughbreds' something else gives
more than it should: the heart the liver

the brain and though it bring in silver
bronze and gold this gift

is a wooden horse whose doors shift
in darkness while grim warriors slip

through your streets with spears lifted
probing for *that* ahh probing for *this* . . .

Shears

For Father's Day they gave me pruning shears
stainless steel with a textured plastic grip
bright red and razor sharp tight springs to hold
the tension   Curved like a scimitar this
weapon a friend observes is made to cut
cojones   All glory be to Allah!
We need an infidel to practice on!

I settle for daisies   Across the road
each mist-wrapped morning the oxeye daisies
open up to light their pure-white nimbi
like ragged stars at dusk popping out in
isolated patches growing thicker
by the minute until there blooms the in-
distinct candescence of the Milky Way

I wade among them a saber-wielding
fever on the move a knee-deep Cancer
snuffing out their brightest lights but trying
not to leave a gaping wound   Their golden
centers echoing the sun each petal's
perfect as a thought of God's or Allah's
geometric and impenetrable

The shears slice through slender stems in silence
until my wrist is tired and my arms
full three vases worth: for the dining room
parlor and piano   For beauty's sake
the music of these daisies floods our home
as silver syllables of *castrati*
broke over holy fathers back in Rome

Black Holes & Einstein

          . . . First they're marble-pale
as Venus flicked in galactic flight
by the thumb of God (you can see a Thumbnail
creasing the curved sky on velvet nights)
Disbelieving the hole's odd behavior
Einstein bet despite his thirty years'
failure to reconcile stone and star
God wouldn't play dice with the universe

He thought the holes too random: our sky
is no lunar love nest or cosmic
jackpot where chips fall where they will   But why
kaleidoscoping through charged fields like shots
lagged in the void do stars collapse and die
making a coffin of space so black and blocked

not even light can escape?   Though now it seems
out of this darkest deck this dense egg
particles spin like roulette wheels wild beams
quarks electrons forming a spectral peg
reuniting the universe fusing
supernova with atom star with stone
telling us there's a rule for everything
under the sun: and everything beyond

Venus green-eyed guide dealer of hands below
whose shaded light more dangerous than
X-rays we study the mysteries if only
you would illumine (for us for Einstein)
Zeus and zero-zero blind luck black holes
                    and if God's a gambling man . . .

II   Stitches

Artist of the Heart

When we were young we couldn't imagine living to be over thirty
nor did we deserve to: everyone chain-smoked drank till we dropped
and drove like suicidal gangsters   Yet here I am at sixty in perfect health
except for fainting once in a while

And you Mother who always lied about your age   confess!
You're eighty-six!   You sit with your cronies playing bridge in permed
respectability still wishing there were men to flirt with
But you've outlived them all sailing your old Buick
across the desert of Orlando like the Queen of Arabia
at twenty miles per hour ignoring all traffic lights

Years ago running off with a piano player how brave you were!
For a woman born in 1960 this would be ordinary even expected
But for a woman born in 1906 this was true courage   O you should be
awarded the President's Medal for Impractical Visionary Valor!

And didn't Harold run over you twice with that same Buick
without breaking a single bone your legs ballooning
like a purple elephant's?   And didn't you throw a TV set
half as large as yourself at our father?   I have often tried to misbehave
as much as you but it's difficult difficult . . .

Did any of this really happen?   We can hardly remember
what we did last Tuesday   Once at a party you drank four martinis
and played Chopin's *Polonaise* with a toothpick in your mouth
not missing a note   Now you get wobbly as a baby on a sliver
of Sacher torte   You can't hold your chocolate anymore

When you had your old face sandpapered it was painful
but you didn't care   Above your cheeks as smooth as Barbie's
your fierce bruised eyes glinted like the Witch of Endor's   *Take that*
Father Time they said you male pig   We were terrified   *That's Grandma*
we told the kids   *She's made some sort of pact*

Still you are the perfect mother you remember everything I tell you
even things I make up are as clear to you as the day they never happened
Each of us is convinced you love us the most how do you do it?
I think you are an artist of the heart   When you enter a room
a secret ray shazams from your withered breast to atomize my knees
On shaky feet I approach you the world slides away
an insubstantial shadow   I am six years old forever
holding out my sticklike arms to you Mother   dearest Mother

Mazzaroli's Cannon

Gods cluster like orgiastic barnacles
along the barrel of this exquisite machine

heating up as shots explode toward flesh
or fortress death aesthetically pleasing

ah, the elegant weapons!
the curved dagger inlaid crossbow the stern

pike manifer and chanfron etched with bands
of delicate tansies   The knuckled anarchy

of art pounds the pursed lips
of common decency   As rows of soldiers

fold in blood vomit excrement
Mazzaroli polishes the brilliant bodies

which he loves not because they're gods
but because they're naked: those muscles

those buttocks the sinews of the neck
the abstract line of back and breast enticing

beyond any responsibility so when
the inevitable bad ending ends he

and all artists shall be ready
with their stunning ivory-crusted
gold-leaf and silvered caskets

Warpath

Poets choose free verse over form one
says because they need room to
belt it out without stone-age three-
edged rules tomahawking their brains before
they get started   For example the five
beat line has been passé since '56

when *Howl* blasted its orgiastic six-
teen gun salvo to freedom without one
shot fired in reply (not counting five
or six palefaced rhymers trying to
hold the fort)   But any poetry for-
mal or free aims at making magic: *Three*

snowy owls swooped down from the North on three
successive nights and *That evening the six-*
fingered Indian was dealing and *I held four*
queens at the stroke of midnight   Everyone
knows that words if they're right are too
slick to be tied to any stake   *If*   I've

sometimes thought all theories are like the Five
Iroquois Tribes ruling New York for three
or thirty or three hundred years doomed to
dust sooner or later like rusty six-
guns no one remembering who won
or lost   Only the words remain neither for

nor against us old arrowheads used for
paperweights   We can sing anything in five
beats or lines or syllables even one
word is enough: *Monongahela*   And three
can make poetry *(Darkling I listen)*   The critic sics
poets on each other like warring tribes to

his own greater glory but the point is to
be able to tell your true story for-
mal as hell or completely free in six
stanzas or none at all: to be able to say *Five*
moons ago we touched under the tall three-
forked tree and the wind and my heart were one

because in art as in life we should line up
our passions single file Indian style with no
tricks: just *one two three four five six*

37

Pissarro Painting 'Young Woman Bathing Her Feet'

Never outline, he told Louis Le Bail—
it only freezes the contours of things.
Paint what's inside, noticing what's around
it, work on everything *simultaneously.*

The young woman's face is flushed
as she soaks her feet in cool green water
The leaves are turning in September light
but sun still soothes the trees

and her hair is wound above her slender
neck   She dreams of the harvest dance
with Lucien though he has said nothing yet
nothing!   She stares at her slim legs

and worries if they're fat   *O time enough*
for the skin to swell for leaves to fall
for the ice to lock like habitual
migraine   But for now her tired feet

revive in the stream dress and petticoat
hiked above pale pink knees as she leans
over the water seeing . . . a pretty young girl
Yes!   the loveliest in all of Louveciennes!

Tolstoy at Yasnaya Polyana

He wanted to be like Jesus
but he was rich and married besides

impediments to sainthood or even
telling the truth   Still he was a genius

whose vision would have been just as just
if written in a peasant's smoky hut

instead of Yasnaya which he loved
for its fields and feathery birch flush

against that house still standing sturdier
than Russia   Yasnaya Polyana molded him as much

as London made Dickens imagine him at dusk
by the cold lake imagining old Bolkonsky

with his wig: *And why should she marry?'* he thought
moving toward the quivering page and us . . .

The Olive Garden

We were waiting lonely in a crowd to be seated
at the Olive Garden when a momentary silence sucked
the heavy strings of background music forward
like a storm across a stand of pines
shaking the nine of us so that a woman in a green hat
suddenly began to cry small shoulders shuddering
earrings bouncing the ceiling light over plastic grapes
clustered on posters of Naples and Rome   We stared
at her while violins called her name and I knew

a hundred years ago some strung-out stranger
in a rented room in Siena wrote this piece
for this exact moment when what he felt
would be felt by someone else in precise proportions
of grief and relief the inward eye seeing a stricken friend
locked in his own head a lovely child gone wrong a father
remote as Mars: everyone in the reception room
understanding this clearly messages absorbed
poco a poco in a rhythmic trance drawing us

together from every race and class as if we could get
along given half a chance and though the waiters happily
didn't sing and the manager maintained a pensive dignity
and no one exactly bared his or her soul
the computer salesman next to us put down
his briefcase and held out his hand
so the woman took it and stood up and they danced
just a few steps before the tables cleared
and we moved on to *pasta e fagiol'*

Easter Recital

for Chris Trakas

I love girls
with little snub noses you sang
in Spanish and I drink to joy you sang
in French and Deep into the bushes of jasmine
you sang in German your baritone brimming
the circular chapel like Noah's flood
while the audience leaned forward
with open mouths as if to pray or say
something of celestial importance
in Latin

and as I stared

behind the
Steinway six arcs of white
chrysanthemums began to bob
and stretch their petals like the wings of doves
until they scored the chapel vaults with oxygen
and we could breathe Mozart and nature and you
combining with such degrees of gracefulness
that corpuscles were kicking in our veins
like a chorus of spring perennials caroling
hosanna

Largo, Maestoso

'Largo, maestoso . . . I don't know' she whispered
'Just think of it as slow and dignified'
Harold needed to know the names of things
and they were listening to a string quartet
by Beethoven called . . . but she forgot
what it was called!   Outside the orange moon
bulged like a full note on an empty staff
She stared out the window with the twin
storms of double bass and violin
stinging her skin like stones

Beethoven she knew had never heard this piece
it howled inside his skull hot and frantic
as a wolf in October erotic
from fingertip to key from bow
to string in passionate
silence   The name was not important
nor the man next to her nor the work
she daily labored on: only the felt
rhythms of grief *lent i lamentand'o*
uniting us below the fretted notes

Prometheus, 1990

Prometheus filches fire over & over
His detractors call him a pyromaniac
in love with the orange flicker the beast
yakking in tongues   He stares into
the changing sameness reading his own story:
passion surging upward unsatisfied consummation

I *am* some kind of weird he thinks liking flames
more than people   *Giver of Wisdom*
Romantic Rebel   Supreme Trickster   as if
I could be anything else!   Unchained
I'd light more fires yes
and chase the howling engines!

My brother looks backward and says
it was my childhood: Clymene our mother spoiled me
I could never relate to authority had
a large appetite and small hands a bad
combination always hungry & needing to prove something
When Zeus said *No* I'd scratch around for matches

I know the future flames ringing the Himalayas
till even my ravenous eagle flies off
and the pyre consumes me at last
The pain has been forever the end certain

And yet the fire warms around it children
huddle:singing

Jonah Caught in a Blizzard

At two A.M. snow rises from the ground
in lazy swirls like a reel run backwards
and they feel they're driving in reverse

lights a vapor trail instead of guide   The car rocks
in gusts the heater quits and to the left a black
Impala glides sideways like a hockey puck

The radio blares *Don't drive!*
His wife: 'You call this driving?'
He's hopped-up as a goalie

the world shrunk to this paperweight
filled with snow and slow motion
that someone holds and shakes like a single die

Rebellious half-believer he suddenly *knows*
'We dwell in a whale's belly wallowing
in miraculous oceans   Chicago will fall'

he tells his wife 'Nineveh's no different than Detroit'
She knows he's bonkers a suburban prophet
howling in the night 'Jonah my dove'

she says 'Whatever   Try not to stall
and when its mouth opens give it the gas'
The lights change and their wheels go round and round

Constellation

for Vaughn Morrison

Our friend names the constellations:
That's Andromeda that's Orion
See there's the Archer there's the Lion
Yes I say not seeing   the stars
prowl randomly through the sky
I stare and stare at no pattern
savage over domestic heads
as we hunt in darkness
on the beach behind our home
Glasses sparkle in our hands the stars
sparkle from expanding distances your eyes
sparkle in starlight and I think

those beams sprinting like spears through
the inside of an African mask
are yes the eyes of gods
watching over us not to love
but to show us we're not alone

there's you

and there's them and there's me

and we are all stars darling
or dreams of stars light spiraling
from our fingers like the rings
of Saturn whirling forever around
the dark rifts between outer and inner

space

The Trashing of Gatlinburg

Beauty is momentary in the mind
but if you're quick you can cash in on it
When rivers flow will fast food lag behind
or Port-o-Potties where the tourists sit?
Americans prefer de Tocqueville said
the useful to the beautiful but if
the beautiful is sold like marmalade
we'll learn to love it cashing in our strips

Still   the Little Pigeon River purls
past rhododendron snowing in the woods
cleansing itself setting an example
we don't follow changing our Good to goods:
while nature and greed like lovers interlock
stretched out in Gatlinburg with greed on top

The Attack

Huffing by the butcher I see my heart
impaled on a hook bloody hunk of fat
venial and menial as a bureaucrat
stumping for reelection   It's an art
this hanging in there past one's prime
until it can't remember why it beats
but just repeats repeats repeats
like an idiot confessing to a crime

I dream I clean it peel it scrub
it to the grain . . . For years I burned
to be pure hard oak but somehow turned
this shapeless lump this tired turnip
humped in rain rooted in mud   Yesterday
at the Gallery I leaned over to see
Pissarro's *La Côte des Boeufs* and something
tore loose inside   I dropped as if to pray

on the dusty floor alarming the passersby
and guard who sat me down
to give me water with reproachful frown:
bad form to die
among the Impressionists
whose flickering canvases urge
us to live more boldly a surge
of sunlight bolting from their wrists

like lightning from God's finger   'Hypo-
glycemia' I told the guard 'I'll be quite
all right . . .' He repeated 'Quite'
but wouldn't let me go
until I swore I wouldn't sue the place
and at last limped out into the winter sun
where a cripple shook his tin of coins
like a dirty fist below my dirty face

The signs for all diseases are the same:
nausea a racing heart cold
sweat: it's boring the old
story except when it's *your* name
on the toe tag   And even then
from a philosophical
point of view it's laughable . . .
so I turn back and enter

the shop   All that meat hanging
there couldn't be more
politically incorrect   My poor
heart whanging
like a shotgun well what the hell:
I look fondly at the ribs the flanks
the patties kidneys glands
chops brains   And bang the bell

Greenhouse Statistics

Four hundred and fifty azaleas
ring our home: a dollhouse dusted
by butterflies   Four hundred we planted
one by delicate one for three decades
cuttings from the original thirty
This perfumed cornucopia spills
ninety-five yards from Big Bayou
where Tampa Bay gapes on the Gulf of Mexico
whose waters rise dark and sure as the shadow
of doom four feet every hundred years
because we love our sweet machines
more than life itself and bring
on rain for us and dust for Northerners:
the good Lord's sense of humor we presume

Our front step stands ten feet above
sea level giving the house they've
just told us two hundred years to go
We should feel safe and yet
impermanence blooms like plaque in the teeth
of our resolve   To rake the lawn
to dig up roots and rocks to sand
window frames and oil the locks
seem somehow not worth it if it all
comes to wreckage in the end   Biblical
prophecies whirl about our heads
drought and flood and famine and disease
gallop in the distance inching toward us
like relentless locusts from the Holy Land

and high above our quiet town
fly Air Force jets with God knows what
payload that could engulf us all
wood and stone marrow and bone
My sweetest dear with whom I've labored
on this house for thirty years
how can we kiss apocalypse?
Because we can imagine our children's
children's children this is no distant
burning out of suns but family
tragedy palpable as Robert
drowning in Frenchman's Creek or pretty
cousin May who left for school
one day and never came home again

Or shouldn't we think about these children
yet to be just hold together as we hold
together now planting azaleas that
outlive us fixing the house because
we love it ignoring the water lapping
at our feet?   Recycle cans refusing plastic
bags?   Embrace our children on the holidays
lugging out the albums once again
to laugh at what we looked like 'way
back when' fondly recalling pets
now long since dead?   But we're not cats
and dogs: looking ahead we'll build
a boat and teach our children's children
how to swim and do the dead man's float

Acorns

Nature stays ahead of us: some
early warning system racing
through fault and root tells it
to up production or shut down
a while so that each year somewhere
often it seems where *we* are
it's the coldest day on record
the rainiest the most snow
the driest March the muggiest
August ever: this year it's acorns

For weeks now in the night winds
of November they've been
pattering our home
like heavenly buckshot a hail
of shrunken stars while we huddle
in hallways echoing Chicken Little
Never so many before!   The oaks sag
and groan beneath their burden   Some say
it's the rains some say it's the Russians
Experts agree it's a premonition of

. . . something   They look Manchurian
these acorns with bland brownish
faces and thatched skullcaps   We
crunch them underfoot like a fifth
world and the air turns bitter
with their broken flesh   Shreds litter
our porches pathways roads
plump birds and squirrels stagger
like drunken looters in Los Angeles   But
everywhere these acorns are digging in

Siamese twins abound yoked
by single stems from a huge oak
shadowing our roof as if
some new dispensation is at hand:
the world will be dark and doubled
twinned roots cracking our sidewalks
and living rooms all the yowling saws
burned out by numbers   Live oaks
water oaks white black the dense
pyramidal pin the noble red . . .

I think they mean: *Time now*
for someone better to take charge
cold-hearted and calm slow to accuse
swaying the world by presence alone
chary of words   We're tired and it's time
for oaks to spread like grass
over the earth's crust curling
cooling healing though even now
deep in the sweetest wood that ever grew
a worm's blind eye blinks its coded message

The First Marriage

for Gretchen and Herb: June 15, 1991

imagine the very first marriage a girl
and boy trembling with some inchoate
need for ceremony a desire for witness:
inventing formality like a wheel or a hoe

in a lost language in a clearing too far from here
a prophet or prophetess intoned to the lovers
who knelt with their hearts cresting
like the unnamed ocean thinking *This is true*

thinking they will never be alone again
though planets slip their tracks and fish
desert the sea repeating those magic sounds
meaning *I do* on this stone below
this tree before these friends *yes* in body
and word my darkdream my sunsong yes *I do I do*

The Secret Code

for Jeanne

Bach was rising from another room

like a secret code in a mathematician's castle
when you came toward me in a summer dress
light slatted through the oaken banister
like a secret code in a mathematician's castle

floating down the stairway in the afternoon
light slatted through the oaken banister
an idea of harmony made manifest
floating down the stairway in the afternoon
striping your slender body like a strobe
an idea of harmony made manifest

The music wound you in a golden braid
striping your slender body like a strobe
and Bach and April and undying youth

like music wound you in a golden braid
conspiring until I knew the dream
of Bach and April and undying youth

would cling across the downward years
conspiring until I knew that dream
despite the disharmonic tarnishing of time
would cling across the downward years
and fuse our lives together like a fugue
to spite the disharmonic tarnishing of time

Then all turned mysterious and blessed
and fused our lives together like a fugue
when you came toward me in a summer dress
turning all mysterious and blessed

while Bach was rising from another room

J

We may not find upon this grainy world
one breathing creature who is incorrupt
Moons drag us all and yet you stand apart
as clear as air have done so since a girl
Not like an unstained child safely curled
in bed or saint with purist heart
swelling in isolation and the doubtless dark:
these prosper selfishly like tidal pearls

But your amazing gentle fingers thrive
among the drifting thimblerigs of error
passion hunger hidden knives   You meet
us on our ground no shell or ivory retreat
here at this strand where light's a spotted mirror
and time's stiff hand floats in at half-past five

Learning Italian

for Kiara

The man is walking with his red dog
How blue the sky is!   I am studying
Italian so I can talk to you my teapot
la mia bella nipotina

Would you like an iced tea?   The bus
is very crowded   We shall visit Parma
in the summer and I shall say
We eat in the kitchen not in the dining room

O that my tongue were younger
and I could sing *A granddaughter*
is a wren in an old man's tree
but instead I shall hold your perfect hand
mispronouncing Will you write many letters?
Here is the spoon   The doctor cannot swim

The Bartok Choir in Castelnuovo

Spotlit at nightfall the pure Hungarian voices rose
toward small stars sprayed like powdered glass
above the church   Their song flew straight up
an acoustical disaster so no one crowded
in the ancient yard could hear a word even
the walls crumbling around us leaned hard
to listen but 'Jubilate Deo' soared like an arrow
toward the ear of God and left us deaf
though not entirely dumb . . .

                             The incessant hum
of muted talk brushed indistinctly by and once
finding a route the music couldn't reach a message
floated through: 'Well I make mine'
a sturdy voice asserted somewhere between
the Bruckner and Poulenc 'with cabbage! . . .'

Castelnuovo's a ghost town its narrow lanes
scraped clear by civilization's savage
instruments some government project never
(of course) completed its population banished
from these heart-bending archways balconies
deep windows tile rooftops in the shadow
of their church and relocated miles away in modern
sleaze: *O when will we rebel where's the lever to pry
this dead hand off?* . . .

                    Now along with these mean
thoughts the smell of *zuppa di cavolo* drifts
through the trees and I see some people near the light
are listening rapt far beyond themselves
as the choir rises to 'Ave Maria' and hunger
is assuaged for a few at least the lucky ones tonight

Campocorto

You spotted snakes with double tongue
Thorny hedgehogs, be not seen;
Newts and blind-worms, do no wrong,
Come not near our fairy queen.
    —*A Midsummer-Night's Dream*

Ants on the moon! you cried and sure enough
crossing its chalk-white surface in a heaven tinged with green
a black ant paused antennae poised scouting
for crumbs along its lunar path   But there was nothing
an ant could bear to earth so it swung
across the sky and landed on the garland of a queen
kneeling in your T-shirt's painted scene
that Shakespeare dreamed four hundred years ago

Even then this home was standing sturdy
as the Duke of Athens' oak stone on stone
rising like destiny its 'short field' nestled
in the mountains now crested
by a daylight moon mirroring your shirt   We
find magic everywhere: this very ant cruising alone
through so much time and space a lucky charm
an insect Puck an actor in your show

Another actor scared you this afternoon:
the snake *Biacco* weaving its way along
the splintered fence   Not all snakes are deadly
and this one thin and green whose slender head
considered us a moment and then slid on
seemed harmless: but what if I were wrong?
Ignorant in Italy I held my tongue
and stroked your hair feeling the silence grow . . .

How can we help the young?   Across America
an army of abandoned children musters in the streets
terrified creatures dangerous and pure
And even here as I watch you pluck with sure
fingers the panicked ant off pale Titania
my heart spins wildly like a frightened leaf
on the mulberry tree where all's still no breeze
at all and yet that one leaf whirls in frantic vertigo

The tree's shadow with its ripe dark fruit
spills on the cobbled wall like silk or wine
It's cooler now   You drop our pilgrim ant
on the darkening ground   Tired or hurt it can't
move fast and stops to stare at a humped root
that turns by the wall into an ivy vine
Above our heads its emerald leaves ignite
gilding the Roman arch of the patio

So much history coded in these stones:
kings have strolled by here inhaling the thick
mild sweetness of the valley huge mounds of gold
ginestre nodding on their spikes   *I'm getting cold*
you say   An evening chill shrivels in my bones
an old man now a sputtering candlestick
The world we're passing on to you is sick
in flesh and spirit but *look!* the valley's all aglow . . .

Your father bends in the garden planting
seven pots of rosemary in a row   The irises
the lilacs all are gone with Titania
and Oberon though in the lane wild strawberries stain
your fingers when they're picked   Everything
in nature can revive even after fire
after flood   Even after man   But now you're tired
The ant's gone too   Child it's time to go

59

Rondini

The breeze leans on the silver chimes just hard
enough to make them audible bubbles
of music like invisible swallows
in the evening air   When you were a child
the light notes of the ice-cream truck blocks away
would make your ears perk up   Now you rock
your own child in her hammock the petals
of her porcelain ears rose-pink in the fading light

Father and daughter awkward prisoners
of our awkward past we sit silent side
by side half dreaming eating cherries picked
this morning gazing idly at the vineyards
the olive trees rising gray as sacrificial
smoke toward a windswept skeptical sky

Above us in the rafters the muddy nests
of swallows balance in each corner   *'Rondine'*
you tell me *'Rondini in the plural'* (God
blessed the birds with pure Italian tongue)
Your book *The Lyre of Orpheus* lies flat
on the footworn stones: we'd like to talk
We couldn't talk for years you and I
we'd face each other daughter-father

across a gap so wide no daredevil
could leap   At least I wasn't brave enough
and howled on the other side like a man
in chains as our first daughter disappeared
as surely as Eurydice went down where even
the notes of Orpheus made no sound

The vines the olive trees twist as if in pain
but still the end is olive oil and wine
Do we have to say *You hurt me there*
or *I was wrong on this?*   Haul the old accusations
to the dock?   The task of Orpheus was clear:
to bring her up to sunlight and not look back
Failing he wept and wandered through the world
alone even the rocks grieving at his songs

And now Kiara stirs   Her quick ears hear
mingling with the chimes the cold high twittering
of swallows who dispatched like messengers
from a land too far to call swoop and loop
across the evening sky scrawling in graceful wing
the Governor's sweet pardon for us all

Fever in Fiesole

Please make fire you piped in your best
English knowing I'd be extravagant
burning expensive wood in that fireplace
large enough for our rented Ford Fiesta

So cold in your stone house!   You shed
sweaters and scarves like goose feathers
scurrying over the brick floor till
we quilted you thickly in your bed

At night the moon hangs low tangled
in stiff branches among silver leaves
and black fruit splintered limbs posing
like frozen dancers stricken and angular

Are you afraid of the dark? your mother asked
bending to kiss and you laughed *Oh no!*
the night's up there it can't come down and hurt me!
your sleeping face pale as an angel mask

Outside the geese two females with one male
lay eggs that never hatch: it's a mystery
At daybreak light-framed you stood already
waiting when their honking woke us all

Buongiorno please   Make fire   I scratch
a match and start it up again   Yesterday's
harsh and crumpled news bursts into flame
Your nose is running   *Naso* I say and touch

the tip wiping it with my sleeve   Then off
we go to feed the geese fresh water
and wilted lettuce   *To keep them from the garden*
your mother says   I wish you wouldn't cough

62

Those geese are tough they even charged the Ford
when we drove in stretching their mottled necks
and waddling toward us like toy tanks in heat
until I swerved and parked across the road

but they follow you like puppies on a leash
. . . And now your mother writes us that you're sick
a blazing fever you can't seem to shake . . .
I wish you were even tougher than your geese

I wish we were there to hear you say *Make fire*
For you I'd torch the entire countryside
and we'd laugh tossing on the olive branches
watching our feathery arms fly faster and higher

III   The Square Root of Love

Counting

We count as simply as we breathe one-

two one-two numbers slipping by like
familiar furniture or that vase

I didn't see for years until you
picked it up   When I was a child
and our cuckoo clock struck three I thought

it was crowing one o'clock three times: one
and one and one is how we start and then
we learn to use our fingers   *How old are you
Peter?* and I'd wiggle four

thumb tucked against my pale pink palm
Our dog Cappy could count to five
Father said clapping five times
before the clever rascal grabbed the bone
but he'd grab it anyway pretty soon

it was a matter of getting
the claps *in* and making the last one *loud*
Unlike Cappy we move from cardinal
to ordinal and only then can count:
he could learn to bark six times
but we know 'six' lies on a rising curve

between five and seven mounting
forever toward that grown-up stage
of love and money connected in ways
they don't teach us as children   What if not
numbers makes dollars and sense of this world?
Even your swaying walk can be measured   I'm
measuring now as you return that vase

3.141592 . . .

. . . and Cetus chained Andromeda until he was slain by Perseus,
who then married her . . .

In school I was attracted
to irrational numbers
stretched out like variable stars

across an expanding void . . .

They're just trouble Miss MacDougall
said trying to lure me back
to *a* over *b* something above zero
we could get hold of

solid as carrots and good for our eyes

but I was a born radical
and hunted numbers salty
as Cetus the sea monster
who waylaid maidens in his
starry lair   I wanted to run

in the wrong circles
like the Princess Andromeda
chained unseen in the skies
of my childhood but whose story
and happy ending I believed
with all my absurd heart because
I longed for something like
the square root of love
which I thought would be

before I passed my prime
permanent and easy as pi . . .

The Math Teacher Tutors His Love

... A point love is a spot in space but
it's hard to pin down   If you want
to make a point you can draw a dot
on a piece of paper like this ...

Only that's not *really* the point just
a picture of it *are you paying attention*
or what?   To complicate things if you use
a #2 pencil like yours that dot
is so thick its number of points
can be infinite and if

your window is open

as it is here (I know it's distracting)
and your paper blows in the breeze *I've got*
it! isn't it now a different point
in a different space?   Still it's the same
in reference to this page but Look
there's no sense in crumpling it up!

... OK I think at this point in time
we can consider the curve and how
we get from *a* to *b* if only you wouldn't
move around *quite* so much ...

Zero

The first time I saw you poised
like Nefertiti on the stairs
I became that obscure Babylonian

mathematician who deep in the Second
Millennium discovered Zero:
in an empty space he placed

the perfect figure

where Mystery and Beauty
intersect and from that point on
the heavens opened up

like a casket of Mesopotamian
rubies and all his calculations
proved correct

Yes, Einstein

There's a hum in my computer
as I write this driving all
other thoughts from my mind
now it's more like a whine: faint
but high pitched hungry and lean
as a headache a nagging voice
a false kiss or

a taint in the blood   Sometimes
I don't hear it but it's still
there like a secret plot making
its subliminal point: life is tedious
like poetry with no sense or passion
just this insidious current
subdivided into waves

small breaths of air expanding
and compressing in a dance
of barbaric repetition
until it breaks upon our ears
a revelation from Humdrum
God of Death. . . . This machine has *got*
to be fixed or thrown out the window!

but just as I grab it
the phone rings and it's you
whispering *Yes Einstein*
yes of course it's me
your words rolling over the dial tone
like Caesar's army building roads
to the capital of the entire world

The Scientist as Gambling Man

When a body exerting force (say yours)
comes in contact with the body
on which this force is exerted (say mine)
we have that branch of physics
called Mechanics: the horse's shoulder
leaning in its harness the jockey's
stirrup bending to the boot   These
are called *contact forces:*   push-pull pull-push

But other forces race through empty space
called *action-at-a-distance forces*
Your weight perfect for the Derby
is a measurement of gravity's attraction
as well as mine   And starshine sprinting
through your hair from distances that terrify
the heart reflects another as does
a rigid compass needling toward true North

Even dreams could they be measured
by their melting instruments have weight
and scope   Those talking numbers beckoning
last night like pimps or touts who know
the world is fixed lie on my morning
like Pimlico's results proclaiming
the low percentage on this earth
of constancy in ordinary bodies

This may be so: a scientific tool
for measuring mechanics of devotion
where the balance of opposing forces
as in revolving doors or starting gates
is measured by a coiled spring and the odds
that we'll emerge from this together
are smaller than the smallest jockey's foot
It may be so: I'll wait to see the proof

Unification Theory

This November evening Lake Norman lies
still as polished aluminum silver surface
brushed by thin bones of dogwood
and sycamore   On the far shore

sweet pine stiffens to stone

From our window we can see
like a shadow on a painting
by Monet a single ripple
tugging the dockpost

where our rowboat's tied

Still   everything moves:
the nuclei of stars click
like iron oarlocks in the wind
and woodboards swell and splinter

to the same laws as any ventricle

vibrated by belief in God
or love some superstring twanging
its heart out to bind us all together
through nightfall and lightfall

here at our picture window on Lake Norman

Acknowledgments

Grateful acknowledgment is made to the following publications in which some of the poems in this collection first appeared: *Abiko Quarterly* ("Artist of the Heart," "Campocorto"); *America* ("Goalfish"); *The Amicus Journal* ("The Trashing of Gatlinburg"); *The Atlantic* ("Scars"); *Black Warrior Review* ("The Bartok Choir at Castelnuovo"); *Clockwatch Review* ("Shears"); *CrossCurrents* ("Jonah Caught in a Blizzard"); *Delos* ("The Vietnamese Fisherman on Tampa Bay"); *Georgia Review* ("Anthills," "The Attack," "The Secret Code," and "Warpath"); *The Greensboro Review* ("Fever in Fiesole"); *The Gryphon* ("Prometheus"); *Heatherstone Press* ("Emily Dickinson in Hell," "Labels, 1972"); *High Plains Literary Review* ("Counting," "3.141592"); *International Quarterly* ("Acorns"); *Kalliope* ("Largo, Maestoso"); *Many Mountains Moving* ("Chinese Wish Poem"); *The New Republic* ("Noreen"); *The Panhandler* ("Blow, Blow, Thou Winter Wind"); *Poetry* ("J," "Mazzaroli's Cannon"); *Slow Dancer* ("Yes, Einstein"); *Snake Nation Review* ("Pissarro Painting *Young Woman Bathing Her Feet*"); *South Florida Poetry Review* ("Reading at Night"); *Southern Humanities Review* ("Tolstoy at Yasnaya Polyana"); *Sow's Ear Poetry Review* ("The Scientist as Gambling Man"); *The Spectator* ("Zero"); *State Street Review* ("Still Life, 1988"); *The Tampa Review* ("Black Holes & Einstein," "Constellation," "Greenhouse Statistics," "Rondini," "Spanish Moss"); *Yankee* ("The First Marriage," "Unnatural Light").

"Learning Italian" first appeared in *The Gettysburg Review* (vol. 9, no. 2), and is reprinted here by permission of the editors.

Thanks also to the University of Hawaii for appointing me visiting writer in fall 1993; to Austin Peay State University in Tennessee for appointing me writer-in-residence in spring 1995; and to the Fine Arts Work Center in Provincetown, Massachusetts, for a master artist's fellowship in September 1995. Many of the poems in this book were written during these residencies.

"Emily Dickinson in Hell" received the 1992 Emily Dickinson Award from the Poetry Society of America. "Scars," "Artist of the Heart," and a small group of other poems received the 1993 Paumanok Poetry Award, sponsored by SUNY/Farmingdale

University. "Campocorto" and a few other poems won the 1995 Sow's Ear Chapbook Competition and were published by the Sow's Ear Press.

And special thanks to Arthur Skinner of Eckerd College for making the slides for the artwork on the covers of both *Scars* and *Liquid Paper*.

Cover art: "Self-Portrait with a Scarf," by Perrie Meinke, 1985.

Peter Meinke was born in Brooklyn, New York, in 1932. He received his A.B. at Hamilton College, his M.A. at the University of Michigan, and his Ph.D. in Literature at the University of Minnesota. His poems and stories have appeared in *The Atlantic, The Georgia Review, The New Republic, Poetry, The New Yorker,* and other magazines. His first book of poems, *The Night Train and the Golden Bird,* was published in the Pitt Poetry Series in 1977; it was followed by *Trying to Surprise God* (1981), *Night Watch on the Chesapeake* (1987), and *Liquid Paper: New & Selected Poems* (1991). His book of stories, *The Piano Tuner,* won the 1986 Flannery O'Connor Award for Short Fiction. A recipient of two poetry fellowships from the National Endowment for the Arts as well as many other awards, he directed the writing workshop at Eckerd College for twenty-seven years, retiring in 1993. Since then he has been writer-in-residence at the University of Hawaii, Austin Peay State University in Tennessee, and the University of North Carolina at Greensboro. He lives in St. Petersburg, Florida, with his wife, the artist Jeanne Clark.

Library of Congress Cataloging-in-Publication Data

Meinke, Peter
    Scars / by Peter Meinke.
        p.   cm. — (Pitt poetry series)
    ISBN 0-8229-3935-5 (cloth : alk. paper). — ISBN 0-8229-5592-X
(paper : alk. paper)
    I. Title. II. Series.
PS3563.E348S27   1996
811' .54—dc20   95-52319